Delving Deeper

A Journey Through Philippians

A Bible Study from the Rooted in the Word Series

By Charissa Jaeger-Sanders

Expedition Journal

DELVING DEEPER:
A JOURNEY THROUGH PHILIPPIANS, EXPEDITION JOURNAL
ISBN-13: 978-1466319325
ISBN-10: 1466319321

www.GraceWorksStudio.org

To those seeking to connect with God deeply and in creative ways. This study is dedicated to and designed for that person who loves to learn. This Journal is for the person who wants to write, doodle, sketch, and scribble his or her way through the Book of Philippians. May Delving Deeper equip you to fully jump into Philippians and engage the text in fresh and profound ways.

Grace and Peace to You,

I am so excited that you have decided to go on this expedition and delve deeper into scripture. Over the next 6 weeks we will be embarking on a journey through Philippians. What will you need to pack for your journey? Bring a Bible, this *Expedition Journal* to write in, a pen, a highlighter, an open heart and mind, and a spirit of adventure.

This Bible study of Philippians requires hard work and close reading. Paying attention to context is key! (Note: The importance of context is true in interpreting any Biblical text.) We will also pay attention to genre. The author of Philippians assumes that the reader/hearer of this epistle has knowledge and understanding of the situation in which and to whom the letter was written. The author also assumes that this letter will be read in its entirety as a book unto itself. The author will not take time to explain the text with footnotes and sidebars; therefore, it is imperative that we take the time to read carefully and try to understand Philippians as it was written in its own time. We will also take time to try and understand the culture and how it would have been interpreted in its original time. Yet, this study will not just be about gaining information for the sake of information. Rather, we will be engaging the text conversationally not only to grow deeper in our understanding of the biblical text, but also to grow deeper in our own relationship with God, in order to transform the way in which we live out our lives as disciples of Jesus Christ. In this journal there is space for grace – space to reflect, to journal, and even space to sketch or doodle. You are invited to use this journal as a means to connect with God and with self.

My hope for you is as you delve deeper into Philippians you will be encouraged, you will be challenged to live more like Christ, and that you will grow in your relationship with Christ. By the end of this study may you be affirmed in what is going well in your relationship with God, may you be challenged to examine your life so that you can learn to live more like Christ, and may you come to know both yourself and God a little better. So let us get started as we delve deeper into Philippians.

In Christ,

Charissa

Using the S.O.A.P.Y. Format

This Bible Study is meant to help you in your spiritual walk. As you begin to integrate Bible Study, reflection and prayer into your life, remember that you will not always do it perfectly. When you miss, there is no need to fret or get discouraged. What is important is that you choose to pick it back up, again. As with any healthy habit it takes time to cultivate it and let it grow to be an extension of yourself. You can opt to light a candle as a way to center yourself and focus on God's presence, acknowledging that it is God's presence that we expect to encounter when we take this time out to read, reflect, and pray. You can do this study in silence or perhaps with some instrumental meditative music in the background. Anything that enables you to draw closer to God is a welcome addition. We will be using a format that uses the acronym S.O.A.P.Y.[i] May this S.O.A.P.Y. Bible Study methodology cleanse our souls as we delve deeper and grow in God's Word!

S – SCRIPTURE: Read the scripture passage aloud so you can hear it. Giving voice to scripture, to the Word of God helps involve more of ourselves. Not only, then, do we use just our eyes, but also our ears and our vocal chords. Reading aloud, also, equips us to slow down, as opposed to skimming over the words, as we might be tempted to do when we read it silently. Allow the words to nurture your spirit as you chew on each one. Highlight, underline or place a mark in the margin next to the scriptures that stand out. When you are done, reread the verses you marked, look for one that particularly spoke to you that day, and write it down.

O - OBSERVATION: Then ask yourself the question: "What is God teaching me/saying to me in this scripture?" As you ask yourself the question, your mind will be full of thoughts. Write down those thoughts. You will know what is being communicated as you reflect upon what you have written. Ask the Holy Spirit to guide you. Then paraphrase – write down in your own words – what this scripture is saying.

A - APPLICATION: Then personalize what you have read by asking yourself how it applies to your life right now. Ask yourself the question, "How does this scripture apply to my life?" Perhaps it is instruction, encouragement, revelation of a new promise, or corrections for a particular area of your life. Write how this scripture can apply to you and your life situation, this week.

P - PRAYER: Then write a prayer to God. The discipline of writing your prayer leads to transformation. This can be as simple as asking God to help you use this scripture, or it may be a greater insight on what God may be revealing to you. Remember, prayer is a two-way conversation, so be sure to take time to listen to what God has to say! And then write down any insights you receive.

Y - YIELDING: As you complete your "S.O.A.P.Y." Bible study, ask yourself the question, "What of my life needs to be yielded to God?" Taking time to answer this question helps lead to complete obedience to God including all aspects of our lives. Each week, through Bible Study, you will have the opportunity to yield a little more of your life to the Lordship of Jesus Christ.

Week 1 (Before the First Class):

Grab a Bible (one that you do not mind writing in) and a pencil and even a highlighter. Read Philippians in its entirety. It is only 4 chapters. I recommend reading it aloud. Read it knowing it is a letter written to the church at Philippi. Read it as a pastoral letter. As you read, notice the themes. Notice what it emphasizes. Also notice its structure. How does it start? In what places do you notice transitions? In the original Greek there would not have been the paragraph divisions that are made in the English translation. These divisions are an interpretation. Feel free to highlight things that strike you. Make notes in the margins on the themes you notice and the structure you see. Familiarize yourself with the book of Philippians as a whole. If you have questions, write them in the margins. As we delve deeper, week-by-week, feel free to ask your questions and to seek answers to your questions. You may even find that answers come in the letter itself. As you go along make your own outline of the text. There is no right or wrong way to make your outline. Your outline should be based off your observations. Where do you see natural divisions? How would you label each section? Are there sub-headings? Do your titles for the headings and sub-headings reflect the major themes that you noticed in the text? In what places do you question or disagree with how it is divided in your Bible?

Outline of Philippians:

When you have finished reading all four chapters and making your own outline of Philippians, look back at your notes and highlights. Prayerfully, pick one or two verses that really struck a chord for you. Write the words of those verses on the S.O.A.P.Y. Reflection Page, and then follow the S.O.A.P.Y. format in order to delve deeper into the scripture passage. You will be using the S.O.A.P.Y. format each week in order to engage the various sections of the Book of Philippians. After the S.O.A.P.Y. pages, there are space for grace pages. Feel free to journal, doodle, and sketch this week during your prayer times and bible study.

S.O.A.P.Y. REFLECTION PAGE

S – SCRIPTURE: _____

_____

_____

_____

O – OBSERVATION: _____

_____

_____

_____

A - APPLICATION: _____

_____

_____

P - PRAYER: _____

_____

_____

_____

Y - YIELDING: _____

_____

_____

Charissa's Outline of the Book of Philippians:

I. Introduction (1:1-11)
 A. Greeting (1:1-2)
 B. Thanksgiving for the Philippians' Participation in the Gospel (1:3-8)
 C. Prayer for the Philippians' Discerning Love to Increase until the Day of Christ (1:9-11)

II. Paul's Current Situation (1:12-26)
 A. Paul's Imprisonment (1:12-13)
 B. The Brothers' Response (1:14-17)
 C. Paul's Attitude (1:18-26)

III. Hands-on Directives in Sanctification[1] (1:27–2:30)
 A. Living Boldly as Citizens of Heaven (1:27–2:30)
 B. Living Humbly as Servants of Christ (2:1-11)
  1. The Motivation to Live Humbly (2:1-4)

---

[1] Sanctification, understood at its core, is the process of growing as a Christian, growing to love God and love neighbor, rightly.

2. The Model of Living Humbly (2:5-11)
    a. Christ's Emptying (2:5-8)
    b. Christ's Exaltation (2:9-11)
C. Living Obediently as Children of God (2:12-18)
    1. The Energizing of God (2:12-13)
    2. The Effect on the Saints (2:14-18)
D. Examples of Humble Servants (2:19-30)
    1. The Example of Timothy (2:19-24)
    2. The Example of Epaphroditus (2:25-30)

IV. Polemical[2] Doctrinal[3] Issues (3:1–4:1)

---

[2] Polemical involves an aggressive attack on or refutation of the opinions or principles of another; it is the art or practice of disputation or controversy (definition taken from http://www.merriam-webster.com/dictionary/polemic)

[3] Doctrinal involves the teaching of a principle or position or the body of principles in a branch of knowledge or system of belief (definition taken from http://www.merriam-webster.com/dictionary/doctrine)

Week 2

DO A CLOSE READING OF PHILIPPIANS 1:1-11:

Paul's Letter to the Philippians[ii]

1:1 Paul and Timothy, servants of Jesus Christ;

To all the saints in Christ Jesus who are at Philippi, with the overseers[4] and servants[5]: 1:2 Grace to you, and peace from God, our Father, and the Lord Jesus Christ. 1:3 I thank my God whenever I remember you, 1:4 always in every request of mine on behalf of you all making my requests with joy, 1:5 for your partnership[6] in furtherance of the Good News from the first day until now; 1:6 being confident of this very thing, that he who began a good work in you will complete it until the day of Jesus Christ. 1:7 It is

---

[4] Or, superintendents, or bishops
[5] Or, deacons
[6] The word translated "partnership" (koinonia) also means "fellowship" and "sharing."

even right for me to think this way on behalf of all of you, because I have you in my heart, because, both in my bonds and in the defense and confirmation of the Good News, you all are partakers with me of grace. 1:8 For God is my witness, how I long after all of you in the tender mercies of Christ Jesus.

1:9 This I pray, that your love may abound yet more and more in knowledge and all discernment; 1:10 so that you may approve the things that are excellent; that you may be sincere and without offense to the day of Christ; 1:11 being filled with the fruits of righteousness, which are through Jesus Christ, to the glory and praise of God.

USE THE S.O.A.P.Y. FORMAT AS A MEANS TO REFLECT ON THIS TEXT. After the S.O.A.P.Y. pages, there are space for grace pages. Feel free to journal, doodle, and sketch this week during your prayer times and bible study.

S.O.A.P.Y. REFLECTION PAGE

S – SCRIPTURE: _____

_____

_____

_____

O – OBSERVATION: _____

_____

_____

_____

A - APPLICATION: _____

_____

_____

P - PRAYER: _____

_____

_____

_____

Y - YIELDING: _____

_____

_____

Week 3

DO A CLOSE READING OF PHILIPPIANS 1:12-26:

1:12 Now I desire to have you know, brothers,[7] that the things which happened to me have turned out rather to the progress of the Good News; 1:13 so that it became evident to the whole palace[8] guard, and to all the rest, that my bonds are in Christ; 1:14 and that most of the brothers in the Lord, being confident through my bonds, are more abundantly bold to speak the word of God without fear. 1:15 Some indeed preach Christ even out of envy and strife, and some also out of good will. 1:16 The former insincerely preach Christ from selfish ambition, thinking that they add affliction to my chains; 1:17 but the latter out of love, knowing that I am appointed for the defense of the Good News.

---

[7] The word for "brothers" here, and where context allows, may also be correctly translated "brothers and sisters" or "siblings."

[8] Or, praetorian

1:18 What does it matter? Only that in every way, whether in pretense or in truth, Christ is proclaimed. I rejoice in this, yes, and will rejoice. 1:19 For I know that this will turn out to my salvation, through your supplication and the supply of the Spirit of Jesus Christ, 1:20 according to my earnest expectation and hope, that I will in no way be disappointed, but with all boldness, as always, now also Christ will be magnified in my body, whether by life, or by death. 1:21 For to me to live is Christ, and to die is gain. 1:22 But if I live on in the flesh, this will bring fruit from my work; yet I don't know what I will choose. 1:23 But I am in a dilemma between the two, having the desire to depart and be with Christ, which is far better. 1:24 Yet, to remain in the flesh is more needful for your sake. 1:25 Having this confidence, I know that I will remain, yes, and remain with you all, for your progress and joy in the faith, 1:26 that your rejoicing may abound in Christ Jesus in me through my presence with you again.

USE THE S.O.A.P.Y. FORMAT AS A MEANS TO REFLECT ON THIS TEXT. After the S.O.A.P.Y. pages, there are space for grace pages. Feel free to journal, doodle, and sketch this week during your prayer times and bible study.

S.O.A.P.Y. REFLECTION PAGE

S – SCRIPTURE: _____

_____

_____

_____

O – OBSERVATION: _____

_____

_____

_____

A – APPLICATION: _____

_____

_____

P – PRAYER: _____

_____

_____

_____

Y – YIELDING: _____

_____

_____

A Covenant Prayer in the Wesleyan Tradition[iii]

I am no longer my own, but thine.
Put me to what thou wilt, rank me with whom thou wilt.
Put me to doing, put me to suffering.
Let me be employed by thee or laid aside for thee,
Exalted for thee or brought low for thee.
Let me be full, let me be empty.
Let me have all things, let me have nothing.
I freely and heartily yield all things to thy pleasure and disposal.
And now, O glorious and blessed God, Father, Son, and Holy Spirit,
Thou art mine, and I am thine. So be it.
And the covenant, which I have made on earth,
Let it be ratified in heaven. Amen.

Week 4

DO A CLOSE READING OF PHILIPPIANS 1:27-2:30:

1:27 Only let your way of life be worthy of the Good News of Christ, that, whether I come and see you or am absent, I may hear of your state, that you stand firm in one spirit, with one soul striving for the faith of the Good News; 1:28 and in nothing frightened by the adversaries, which is for them a proof of destruction, but to you of salvation, and that from God. 1:29 Because it has been granted to you on behalf of Christ, not only to believe in him, but also to suffer on his behalf, 1:30 having the same conflict which you saw in me, and now hear is in me.

2:1 If there is therefore any exhortation in Christ, if any consolation of love, if any fellowship of the Spirit, if any tender mercies and compassion, 2:2 make my joy full, by being like-minded, having the same love, being of one accord, of one mind; 2:3 doing nothing through rivalry or through conceit, but in humility, each counting others better than himself; 2:4 each of you not just looking to his own things, but each of you also to the things of others.

2:5 Have this in your mind, which was also in Christ Jesus, 2:6 who, existing in the form of God, didn't consider equality with God a thing to be grasped, 2:7 but emptied himself, taking the form of a servant, being made in the likeness of men. 2:8 And being found in human form, he humbled himself, becoming obedient to death, yes, the death of the cross. 2:9 Therefore God also highly exalted him, and gave to him the name which is above every name; 2:10 that at the name of Jesus every knee should bow, of those in heaven, those on earth, and those under the earth, 2:11 and that every tongue should confess that Jesus Christ is Lord, to the glory of God the Father.

2:12 So then, my beloved, even as you have always obeyed, not only in my presence, but now much more in my absence, work out your own salvation with fear and trembling. 2:13 For it is God who works in you both to will and to work, for his good pleasure. 2:14 Do all things without murmurings and disputes, 2:15 that you may become blameless and harmless, children of God without blemish in the midst of a crooked and perverse generation, among whom you are seen as lights in the world, 2:16 holding up the word of life; that I may have something to boast in the day of Christ, that I didn't run in vain nor labor in vain. 2:17 Yes, and if I am poured out on the sacrifice and service of your faith, I rejoice, and rejoice with you all. 2:18 In the same way, you also rejoice, and rejoice with me.

2:19 But I hope in the Lord Jesus to send Timothy to you soon, that I also may be cheered up when I know how you are doing. 2:20 For I have no one else like-minded, who will truly care about you. 2:21 For they all seek their own, not the things of Jesus Christ. 2:22 But you know the proof of him, that, as a child serves a father, so he served with me in furtherance of the Good News. 2:23 Therefore I hope to send him at once, as soon as I see how it will go with me. 2:24 But I trust in the Lord that I myself also will come shortly. 2:25 But I counted it necessary to send to you Epaphroditus, my brother, fellow worker, fellow soldier, and your apostle and servant of my need; 2:26 since he longed for you all, and was very troubled, because you had heard that he was sick. 2:27 For indeed he was sick, nearly to death, but God had mercy on him; and not on him only, but on me also, that I might not have sorrow on sorrow. 2:28 I have sent him therefore the more diligently, that, when you see him again, you may rejoice, and that I may be the less sorrowful. 2:29 Receive him therefore in the Lord with all joy, and hold such in honor, 2:30 because for the work of Christ he came near to death, risking his life to supply that which was lacking in your service toward me.

USE THE S.O.A.P.Y. FORMAT AS A MEANS TO REFLECT ON THIS TEXT. After the S.O.A.P.Y. pages, there are space for grace pages. Feel free to journal, doodle, and sketch this week during your prayer times and bible study.

S.O.A.P.Y. REFLECTION PAGE

S – SCRIPTURE: _____

_____

_____

_____

O – OBSERVATION: _____

_____

_____

_____

A - APPLICATION: _____

_____

_____

P - PRAYER: _____

_____

_____

_____

Y - YIELDING: _____

_____

_____

Week 5

DO A CLOSE READING OF PHILIPPIANS 3:1-4:1:

3:1 Finally, my brothers, rejoice in the Lord. To write the same things to you, to me indeed is not tiresome, but for you it is safe. 3:2 Beware of the dogs, beware of the evil workers, beware of the false circumcision. 3:3 For we are the circumcision, who worship God in the Spirit, and rejoice in Christ Jesus, and have no confidence in the flesh; 3:4 though I myself might have confidence even in the flesh. If any other man thinks that he has confidence in the flesh, I yet more: 3:5 circumcised the eighth day, of the stock of Israel, of the tribe of Benjamin, a Hebrew of Hebrews; concerning the law, a Pharisee; 3:6 concerning zeal, persecuting the assembly; concerning the righteousness which is in the law, found blameless.

3:7 However, what things were gain to me, these have I counted loss for Christ. 3:8 Yes most certainly, and I count all things to be loss for the excellency of the knowledge of Christ Jesus, my Lord, for whom I suffered the loss of all things, and count them nothing but refuse, that I may gain Christ 3:9 and be found in him, not having a righteousness of my own, that which is of the law, but that which is through faith in Christ, the righteousness which is from God by faith; 3:10 that I may know him, and the power of his resurrection, and the fellowship of his sufferings, becoming conformed to his death; 3:11 if by any means I may attain to the resurrection from the dead. 3:12 Not that I have already obtained, or am already made perfect; but I press on, if it is so that I may take hold of that for which also I was taken hold of by Christ Jesus.

3:13 Brothers, I don't regard myself as yet having taken hold, but one thing I do. Forgetting the things which are behind, and stretching forward to the things which are before, 3:14 I press on toward the goal for the prize of the high calling of God in Christ Jesus. 3:15 Let us therefore, as many as are perfect, think this way. If in anything you think otherwise, God will also reveal that to you. 3:16 Nevertheless, to the extent that we have already attained, let us walk by the same rule. Let us be of the same mind. 3:17 Brothers, be imitators together of me, and note those who walk this way, even as you have us for an example. 3:18 For many walk, of whom I told you often, and now tell you even weeping, as the enemies of the cross of Christ, 3:19 whose end is destruction, whose god is the belly, and whose glory is in their shame, who think about earthly things. 3:20 For our citizenship is in heaven, from where we also wait for a Savior, the

Lord Jesus Christ; 3:21 who will change the body of our humiliation to be conformed to the body of his glory, according to the working by which he is able even to subject all things to himself.

4:1 Therefore, my brothers, beloved and longed for, my joy and crown, so stand firm in the Lord, my beloved.

USE THE S.O.A.P.Y. FORMAT AS A MEANS TO REFLECT ON THIS TEXT. After the S.O.A.P.Y. pages, there are space for grace pages. Feel free to journal, doodle, and sketch this week during your prayer times and bible study.

S.O.A.P.Y. REFLECTION PAGE

S – SCRIPTURE: _____

_____

_____

_____

O – OBSERVATION: _____

_____

_____

_____

A ~ APPLICATION: _____
_____
_____

P ~ PRAYER: _____
_____
_____

Y ~ YIELDING: _____
_____
_____

Week 6

DO A CLOSE READING OF PHILIPPIANS 4:2-23:

4:2 I exhort Euodia, and I exhort Syntyche, to think the same way in the Lord. 4:3 Yes, I beg you also, true yokefellow, help these women, for they labored with me in the Good News, with Clement also, and the rest of my fellow workers, whose names are in the book of life. 4:4 Rejoice in the Lord always! Again I will say, "Rejoice!" 4:5 Let your gentleness be known to all men. The Lord is at hand. 4:6 In nothing be anxious, but in everything, by prayer and petition with thanksgiving, let your requests be made known to God. 4:7 And the peace of God, which surpasses all understanding, will guard your hearts and your thoughts in Christ Jesus.

4:8 Finally, brothers, whatever things are true, whatever things are honorable, whatever things are just, whatever things are pure, whatever things are lovely, whatever things are of good report; if there is any virtue, and if there is any praise, think about these things. 4:9 The things which you learned, received, heard, and saw in me: do these things, and the God of peace will be with you. 4:10 But I rejoice in the Lord greatly, that now at length you have revived your thought for me; in which you did indeed take thought, but you lacked opportunity. 4:11 Not that I speak in respect to lack, for I have learned in whatever state I am, to be content in it. 4:12 I know how to be humbled, and I know also how to abound. In everything and in all things I have learned the secret both to be filled and to be hungry, both to abound and to be in need. 4:13 I can do all things through Christ, who strengthens me. 4:14 However you did well that you shared in my affliction. 4:15 You yourselves also know, you Philippians, that in the beginning of the Good News, when I departed from Macedonia, no assembly shared with me in the matter of giving and receiving but you only. 4:16 For even in Thessalonica you sent once and again to my need. 4:17 Not that I seek for the gift, but I seek for the fruit that increases to your account. 4:18 But I have all things, and abound. I am filled, having received from Epaphroditus the things that came from you, a sweet-smelling fragrance, an acceptable and well-pleasing sacrifice to God. 4:19 My God will supply every need of yours according to his riches in glory in Christ Jesus. 4:20 Now to our God and Father be the glory forever and ever! Amen.

4:21 Greet every saint in Christ Jesus. The brothers who are with me greet you. 4:22 All the saints greet you, especially those who are of Caesar's household. 4:23 The grace of the Lord Jesus Christ be with you all. Amen.

USE THE S.O.A.P.Y. FORMAT AS A MEANS TO REFLECT ON THIS TEXT. After the S.O.A.P.Y. pages, there are space for grace pages. Feel free to journal, doodle, and sketch this week during your prayer times and bible study.

S.O.A.P.Y. REFLECTION PAGE

S – SCRIPTURE: _____

_____

_____

_____

O – OBSERVATION: _____

_____

_____

_____

A - APPLICATION: _____

_____

_____

P – PRAYER: _____

_____

_____

_____

Y – YIELDING: _____

_____

_____

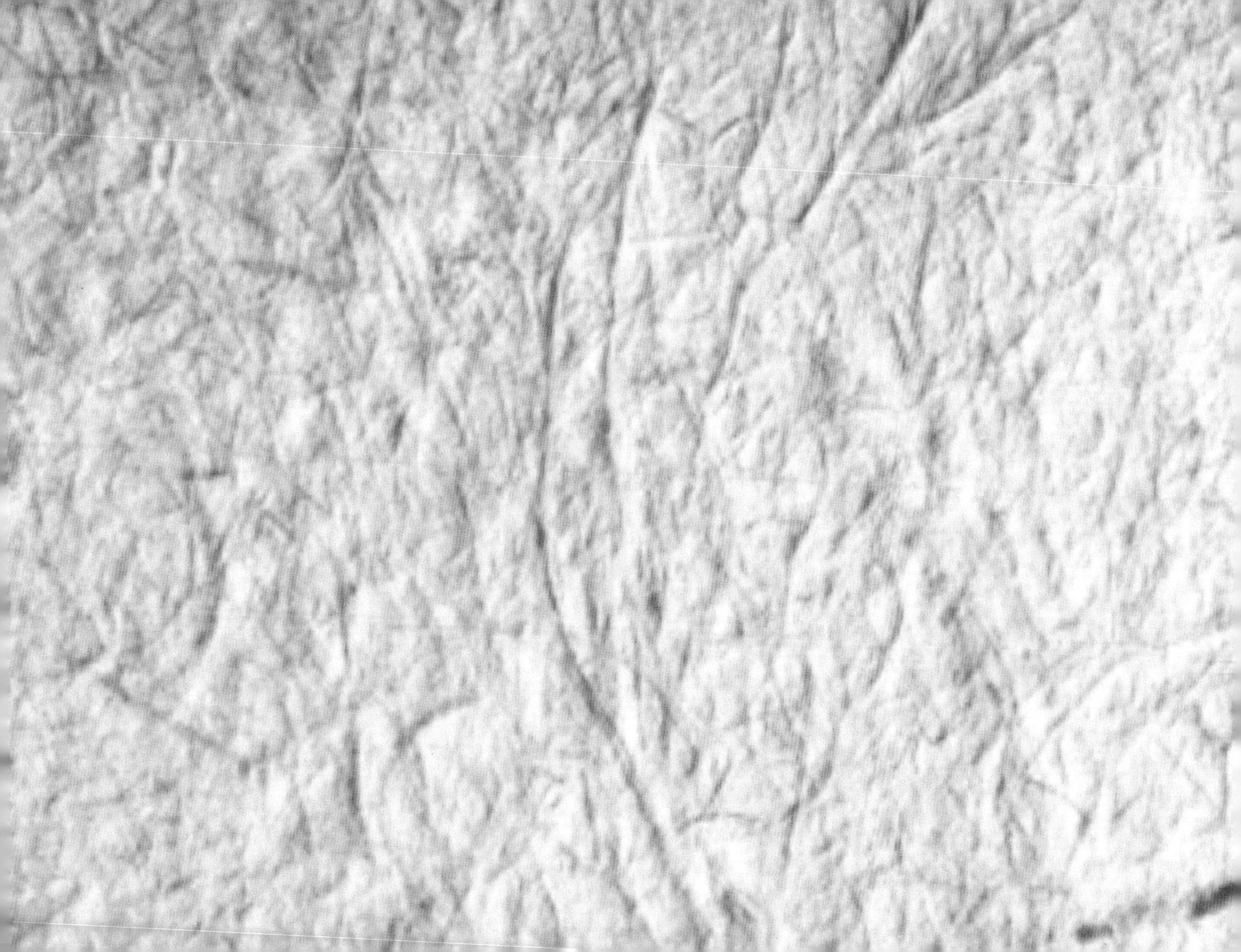

Map ^{iv}

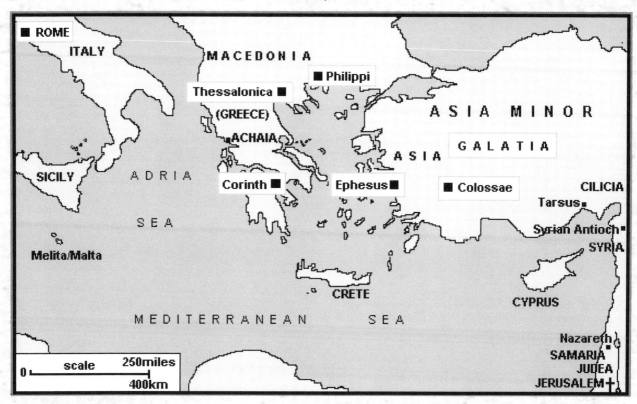

ROME
ITALY
MACEDONIA
Philippi
Thessalonica
(GREECE)
ASIA MINOR
ACHAIA
GALATIA
ASIA
SICILY
ADRIA
Corinth
Ephesus
Colossae
CILICIA
Tarsus
SEA
Syrian Antioch
SYRIA
Melita/Malta
CYPRUS
CRETE
MEDITERRANEAN   SEA
Nazareth
SAMARIA
JUDEA
JERUSALEM

scale   250miles
0   400km

About the Author

Charissa served as a United Methodist Pastor in congregational ministry for over 6½ years. Charissa is now an ordained deacon of the United Methodist Church as well as a professional artist. She integrates these two passions into the work of Grace Works Studio. She uses art as a means of grace and engages art in Bible studies, retreat settings, devotionals, contemplative worship, and as a way to reach at risk communities. Through art, Charissa facilitates a unique way to connect with God, with self, and with others. Charissa now serves as the founder and director of Grace Works Studio, LLC.

Raised in Tallahassee, Florida, Charissa now lives in Lady Lake with her husband, Chris and their two dogs, Jessie and Molly.

To learn more about Charissa and the ministry that she does, please visit her website at www.GraceWorksStudio.org.

About the Artwork

The cover art was done by Charissa Jaeger-Sanders. This watercolor painted on canvas is entitled *Rooted in the Word*. The concept of *Rooted in the Word* is grounded in writing Bible Studies that are in depth and deeply connected to the biblical text, while integrating hands on and artistic components that allow us to connect with God, self, and one another on a different level. The artwork used at the beginning of each chapter is also by Charissa Jaeger-Sanders; it is entitled *Grounded in Love* (Charcoal, Black India Ink, Graphite, and White Pastel Stick on Watercolor Paper). May our lives be rooted and grounded in the love and presence of God, and may God use us as vessels filling us and pouring us out for God's work in the world.

Endnotes:

---

[i] The S.O.A.P.Y. format is adapted from: http://www.fumcpeoria.org/grow/soapybiblestudy.asp

[ii] Scripture passages used in this journal are from the World English Bible (WEB), a public domain (no copyright) modern English translation of the Holy Bible. The World English Bible is based on the American Standard Version (ASV) of the Bible, the Biblia Hebraica Stutgartensa Old Testament, and the Greek Majority Text New Testament. You are welcome to read another translation/version, as well. I recommend the NRSV or NIV as good additional translations. The passages are included for your convenience.

[iii] *The United Methodist Hymnal.* Nashville: Abingdon Press, 1989. No. 607

[iv] Map taken from http://www.ccel.org/bible/phillips/CN092MAPS1.htm; another good source for biblical maps is Pritchard, James B., ed. *The Harper Collins Concise Atlas of the Bible.* London: Time Books, 1991. Page 120 and 121.

Made in the USA
Lexington, KY
20 August 2016